Merry Misfits: A Hilarious Guide to Non-Traditional Christmas Party Chaos

Tropical Christmas Party Ideas, Unconventional Celebrations, and Outrageous Games to Ensure Your Holiday's a Hot Mess (in the Best Way Possible)

Celebration Chaos Chronicles
Book 1

Bree Winterson

Copyright © 2024 by Bree Winterson

All rights reserved.

No part of this book may be reproduced in any form or by any electronic or mechanical means, including information storage and retrieval systems, without written permission from the author, except for the use of brief quotations in a book review.

Contents

Sleigh Bells & Sandcastles: Your Wild Ride to a Tropical Christmas Bashcal Christmas Madness — v

1. Deck the Palms – Tropical Holiday Decor — 1
2. Unconventional Party Themes – Because Normal is Overrated — 7
   "Santa Goes South" Party — 9
   "Christmas at the Beach" Party — 13
   "Tacky Luau Christmas" — 15
   Pro Tips for Pulling Off an Unconventional Christmas Party — 17
3. Offbeat Christmas Games – Fun, Festive, and Ridiculously Entertaining — 19
   Santa's Flamingo Toss — 21
   Elf Limbo — 23
   Christmas Coconut Bowling — 25
   Snowball Toss — 27
   Ho-Ho-Hula Dance-Off — 29
   Reindeer Ring Toss — 31
   Holiday Piñata Smash — 33
   Naughty or Nice Trivia — 35
4. Tropical-Inspired Christmas Treats – Sweet, Sunny, and Totally Delicious — 37
   Grilled Pineapple Santa Skewers — 39
   Coconut Snowballs — 41
   Christmas Nachos — 43
   Tropical Fruitcake — 45
   Mango & Papaya Christmas Salsa — 47
   Key Lime Pie Christmas Bars — 49
   Rum-Soaked Christmas Pudding — 51
5. Fun Twists on Holiday Traditions – Redefining the Christmas Spirit — 53

Tropical Secret Santa	55
Christmas Karaoke – Island Style	57
Rudolph's Surfing Challenge	59
Island Gift Wrapping Contest	61
Beach Blanket Christmas Movie Marathon	63
6. Humorous Holiday Disasters – What Could Go Wrong?	65
The Palm Tree Tipping Incident	67
The Inflatable Santa Blowout	69
Escape the Heat – Surviving a Christmas Heatwave	71
The Sand-in-the-Socks Debacle	73
7. Gifts No One Wants (But Everyone Will Laugh About)	75
8. Santa's Outrageous Outfits – Dressing the Jolly Old Elf for the Tropics	83
Santa Claus in a Hawaiian Shirt	85
Reindeer with Sunglasses	87
Santa's Lifeguard Look	89
Mrs. Claus Goes to the Beach	91
Elf on Vacation	93
Frosty the Surfer Snowman	95
Reindeer Lifeguard Team	97
9. The Aftermath – Cleaning up After the Tropic Christmas	99
How to Remove Sand from Your Living Room	101
Dealing with Too Much Pineapple	103
Tackling the Tiki Torch Disaster	105
Deflating Santa and His Reindeer	107
The Coconut Drink Dilemma	109
Dealing with the Leftover Decorations	111
Sand, Sunburn, and Santa's Hawaiian Shirt: You Survived the Madness!	113
From the Desk of Bree Winters: Surviving Christmas, One Piña Colada at a Time	115

Sleigh Bells & Sandcastles: Your Wild Ride to a Tropical Christmas Bashcal Christmas Madness

So, you've found yourself holding a book about throwing a *tropical-themed* Christmas party. Let that sink in for a second. A tropical Christmas! As if the holidays weren't already wild enough, we're going to toss in palm trees, coconuts, and inflatable flamingos right next to Santa's sleigh. And you, brave reader, are along for the ride. Buckle up—it's going to be a sunburned, piña colada-filled sleigh ride like no other!

Let's face it: traditional Christmas parties can get a little predictable. The same decorations, the same carols, the same food that leaves you questioning whether you've accidentally slipped into a turkey coma. But not *this* year. Oh no, *this* year, you're turning up the heat—literally—with sand in your stockings and Santa in Bermuda shorts.

You see, this book isn't just a guide to throwing a party; it's your ultimate survival kit for creating the most chaotic, hilarious, and possibly regrettable holiday experience of your life. You'll find yourself wondering, "Did I really just read a chapter on how to deflate an inflatable reindeer?" Yes. Yes, you did. And guess what? That's just the beginning. You've signed up for a Christmas adventure filled with palm trees that tip over, reindeer with sunglasses, and enough leftover pineapple to start your own juice company.

But here's the thing—every epic party needs a little chaos. What's a tropical Christmas without a flamingo flying off the lawn or a "Merry Margarita" punch that takes down half your guests? We'll guide you through it all, from the disastrous cleanup of sand (spoiler: it's everywhere) to the joy of watching Santa try to navigate a surfboard in flip-flops. You'll laugh, you'll cry (mostly from laughing too hard), and you might even wonder why you ever thought this was a good idea in the first place.

By the end of this book, you'll be fully prepared to pull off a Christmas party like no other—a Christmas where Rudolph might be wearing sunscreen and Mrs. Claus is sipping a piña colada on a pool float.

So, grab your sunblock and your ugliest Hawaiian shirt. You're about to embark on a festive journey filled with palm trees, pineapples, and holiday disasters you'll be telling stories about for years. This isn't just Christmas. This is *tropical*Christmas, and trust me, you won't want to miss a single sun-soaked, snow-free moment of it.

Are you ready? Let's make some (questionable) Christmas magic. Cheers to a holiday that's totally off the rails!

Deck the Palms – Tropical Holiday Decor

Welcome to your first stop on the road to **Christmas rebellion!** If the sight of snow makes you want to grab your suitcase and hop on the next flight to the Caribbean, then you're in the right place. This chapter is dedicated to transforming your home into a tropical Christmas paradise—think less "Winter Wonderland" and more "Island Oasis with a dash of Christmas spirit." We're ditching the sleigh and hopping on a surfboard, because who needs reindeer when you've got flamingos?

CHRISTMAS IN THE TROPICS: Ditch Frosty the Snowman for Flip-Flop Santa

Why settle for the same ol' winter wonderland when you can crank up the heat and swap snowflakes for sunshine? It's time to trade in your scarves and mittens for sunscreen and shades, and bring some tropical flare to your Christmas festivities. Forget the pine trees and chilly vibes—this holiday, we're decking the halls with palm leaves, coconuts, and a whole lot of flamingo-themed fun. Let's dive into how to turn your home into a sun-soaked Christmas paradise!

PALM TREES, Not Pine Trees: Tropi-Fy Your Holiday Decor

If you're still clinging to the idea that Christmas trees need to be evergreens, it's time to step out of the snowbank and into the sand. We're taking that "deck the halls" phrase literally, and those halls are going to look like the set of *Moana* meets Santa's workshop.

PALM LEAVES FOR TINSEL? Why Not! Palm leaves—hear me out. These guys don't get enough love. Drape them like tinsel around your fireplace, over your dining table, or even—brace yourself—your Christmas tree. Don't stop there! Add some fairy lights for that tropical holiday glow and, if you're feeling festive (and mildly chaotic), spray-paint those bad boys in Christmas colors. Red and green glitter palm garlands? That's the kind of decision that says, "I might be losing my mind, but it's a party."

HIBISCUS OVER HOLLY Holly and poinsettias are cute, but they scream "snowy cabin," and you're aiming for "beach bungalow."

Grab some hibiscus flowers—real or fake, who's checking?—and scatter them around the house. Put a few in vases, tuck one behind your ear for that "I'm totally running this tropical tour" look, or use them as placeholders on your Christmas dinner table. Bonus points if you work the word "aloha" into your holiday greetings.

The Palm Tree Christmas Tree: The Ultimate Holiday Glow-Up

Why settle for a traditional Christmas tree when you can have a palm tree that doesn't leave needles all over the floor? This year, it's time to get creative, and if you're looking for an excuse to finally have a Christmas tree that doesn't involve vacuuming every 20 minutes, look no further.

Inflatable Palm Tree—Low Maintenance, High Sass

Let me introduce you to your new best friend: the inflatable palm tree. It's big, it's bold, and it requires zero watering. You can find these party showstoppers at most stores, and once you've got it home, it's game on. Decorate it with flamingo ornaments (yes, they're a thing), tiki lights, and a starfish on top. Feeling extra wild? Throw in a couple of inflatable parrots and let them oversee present distribution.

Real Palm Trees—For the Overachievers

If you're lucky enough to live somewhere warm, or if you've somehow managed to keep a palm tree alive in your living room, then congrats—you're winning Christmas. Drape your palm in seashell garlands, hang mini surfboards as ornaments, and crank up "Mele Kalikimaka" while you decorate. Who needs snow when you can have coconuts and tropical beats?

. . .

Pineapples: The Christmas Mascots You Didn't Know You Needed

Let's talk centerpieces—because nothing says tropical Christmas like pineapples. We're going to take these spiky fruits and turn them into your holiday table's MVP. Ready?

Pineapple Santas: Tropical, Yet Festive First, you're going to need some pineapples. Now, plop tiny Santa hats on top of each one and boom—you've got yourself a pineapple Santa brigade. If you're feeling extra fancy, draw little faces on them or give them sunglasses for that "Santa's on vacation" vibe. Surround them with a rainbow of tropical fruits—mangoes, papayas, and coconuts—and you've got a table that screams "Christmas in paradise."

Coconut Drink Cups: Sip in Style

No holiday party is complete without a beverage station that makes your guests do a double-take. And since you're going tropical this year, plain ol' cups just won't do. Time to break out the coconuts!

Coconut Drink Cups—Pure Genius Scoop out some coconuts (or buy the plastic ones, we don't judge) and serve up your cocktails in true island fashion. Stick in a tiny umbrella and a candy cane stirrer, and suddenly, that rum punch feels like it belongs on a beach. The only snowflakes at this party are the coconut flakes you might use to garnish the drinks.

. . .

Snow? Who Needs It When You Have Sand!

Let's face it, snow is overrated. It's cold, wet, and makes everyone cranky. Sand, on the other hand, is soft, warm, and makes you feel like you're on vacation. So this Christmas, we're bringing the beach indoors without the annoying bits that get stuck in your socks.

Sand > Snow Who needs fake snow when you can sprinkle decorative sand across your tabletops and windowsills? Create a tiny beach diorama on your coffee table—add some seashells, mini umbrellas, and a few plastic crabs to really set the scene. It's like a winter wonderland, except no one's freezing their toes off.

Seashell Wreaths—Goodbye Pinecones, Hello Conch Give your front door the tropical treatment with a DIY seashell wreath. Grab a bunch of seashells (go collect them if you want an excuse to take a vacation) and glue them to a wreath base. For a little extra flair, dust some of the shells with gold or silver paint, or add a string of mini lights. Your neighbors will be torn between jealousy and confusion, but at least you'll have the best-dressed door on the block.

Santa Swaps His Boots for Flip-Flops

Santa's tired of trudging through snow in those heavy black boots. This year, he's showing up in board shorts, a Hawaiian shirt, and—you guessed it—flip-flops.

Surfing Santa Figurines Why stop at Santa in flip-flops when you can have Santa catching waves? If you can't find a figurine of

Santa shredding a gnarly wave, make your own. Grab an old Santa figurine, glue a tiny surfboard to his feet, and let him ride those yuletide swells under your palm tree Christmas tree.

SURFBOARD CHRISTMAS TREE: Go Big or Go Home

Are you feeling bold? Skip the tree entirely and go for a surfboard-shaped Christmas tree. Yes, really.

SURFBOARD FESTIVITIES LEAN your surfboard against the wall and wrap it in lights and garlands. No surfboard? No problem! Cut one out of cardboard, paint it with tropical patterns, and you've just created a Christmas tree that says, "I may not surf, but I know how to party."

BY THE TIME you're done, your home will look like Santa's tropical vacation retreat, and your guests will be wondering why they ever bothered with cold weather in the first place. So sit back, sip your coconut cocktail, and enjoy the beachiest, most sun-soaked Christmas celebration your friends have ever seen. Who needs sleigh bells when you've got steel drums?

Now, what's next? Unconventional party themes and tropical Christmas games, of course! But for now, bask in the glow of your pineapple Santas and inflatable palm trees. Merry Christmas—and don't forget the sunscreen!

Unconventional Party Themes – Because Normal is Overrated

Let's face it: traditional Christmas parties can be a bit predictable. You've got the same old tinsel, the same reindeer sweaters, and yet another bowl of eggnog. While we love a good ugly sweater moment, it's time to shake things up. This chapter is all about embracing the unexpected, turning the holiday on its head, and throwing a party that no one will forget (mostly because they'll be too busy laughing).

We're merging tropical vibes with holiday cheer for a party experience that's far from ordinary. If you've ever wondered what happens when Santa trades in his sleigh for a surfboard, this is your moment. Unconventional themes are your chance to bring a little sunshine to your Christmas celebration, sprinkle in some silliness, and throw tradition out the window—where it can hang out with the snow you no longer need.

"Santa Goes South" Party

Theme Overview:

Santa's not always about the cold. In this version, he's relaxing in a beach chair, sipping a piña colada, and probably wearing SPF 50. The "Santa Goes South" party is a tropical vacation with a holiday twist, where Hawaiian shirts replace sweaters and flip-flops are totally acceptable Christmas footwear. Get ready for some island vibes with a side of jingle bells.

Dress Code:

Encourage your guests to get in on the fun! The dress code is simple: think tropical vacation meets North Pole. Hawaiian shirts paired with Santa hats, sunglasses, and flip-flops are the perfect combination. Want to take it a step further? Hand out bonus points for the guest who shows up with a faux sunburn or a Christmas-themed swimsuit.

Decor Ideas:

Set the scene by transforming your party space into a beachy winter wonderland. Wrap palm trees (real or inflatable) in Christmas lights and swap the traditional fireplace for tiki torches adorned with festive red bows. Throw in inflatable flamingo decorations and scattered seashells to really bring the theme home. For a quirky touch, use surfboards and beach balls with holiday designs to double as both decor and props for photo ops.

Food & Drinks:

No tropical party is complete without some fun, festive drinks! Serve tropical cocktails with a holiday twist:

- **Merry Margaritas**: Classic margaritas, but give them a Christmas twist by garnishing with cranberries and mint.
- **Jingle Juice**: A festive piña colada that brings the tropics to your holiday celebration.
- **Rudolph's Rum Punch**: A fruity, rum-based punch that will have guests feeling warm and fuzzy inside, no matter the weather outside.

For snacks, keep it light and beachy with coconut shrimp, pineapple salsa, and Christmas cookies shaped like palm trees. Add a tropical fruit platter for good measure, and watch as your guests snack their way to paradise.

Party Activities:

Get ready to swap your usual Secret Santa exchange for some island-inspired fun:

- **Coconut Bowling**: Set up a row of plastic flamingo pins and let your guests bowl with coconuts. It's more challenging than it sounds, and way more hilarious.

- **Tropical Carol Karaoke**: Invite your guests to belt out Christmas classics—tropical style. Think "Deck the Palms" or "Mele Kalikimaka" instead of "Deck the Halls." Bonus points for anyone brave enough to sing while wearing a lei and flip-flops!

"Christmas at the Beach" Party

Theme Overview:
If you're longing for the beach but stuck in the middle of winter, this party is your chance to bring the sand and sun to your celebration—whether you're indoors or in a warm locale. It's all about creating that perfect blend of summer vibes and holiday cheer. Picture Santa in a lifeguard chair, sunglasses on, ready to make some waves.

Dress Code:
Let's crank up the heat (literally). Your guests should come decked out in swimsuits, flip-flops, and beach hats, no matter if it's indoors. And don't forget the Santa hats to keep things festive! For those feeling extra bold, encourage holiday-themed bathing suits—because nothing says "Merry Christmas" like Rudolph on a speedo.

Decor Ideas:
Transform your space into a seaside escape with beach towels spread across the floor, colorful beach umbrellas, and small decorative sandboxes or vases filled with sand. Create a faux beach

bonfire by stacking logs wrapped in red ribbon and surrounding them with twinkle lights. The soft glow will give the illusion of a warm, beachy fire, perfect for an indoor Christmas luau.

Food & Drinks:

Stay true to the beach party theme with fresh, light fare:

- **Watermelon Slices**: Serve in fun holiday shapes like Christmas trees and stars.
- **Grilled Fish Tacos**: Add some spice with a tropical twist.
- **Snow Cones**: Dye them red and green for a festive touch.

For drinks, you can't go wrong with **Frosty's Frozen Daiquiri**—a fun and frosty take on the classic frozen daiquiri. Blend them up in different holiday colors and serve with mini candy canes for stirrers.

Party Activities:

- **Pool Float Reindeer Races**: If you've got a pool, this activity is a must! Have guests hop on inflatable reindeer floats and race across the water. No pool? No problem! Set up a mock race inside by using the inflatables and cheering them on as they waddle around the room.
- **Beach Ball Volleyball**: Play a casual game of volleyball using an inflatable beach ball decorated with holiday patterns. It's a fun way to add a bit of movement to your party without requiring guests to break a sweat—unless they really want to win.

"Tacky Luau Christmas"

Theme Overview:

Who says ugly Christmas sweaters have to be the star of the show? At the "Tacky Luau Christmas" party, we're taking things to the next level by combining the worst of holiday fashion with luau kitsch. The result? A glorious, mismatched, tacky explosion that's guaranteed to get a laugh.

Dress Code:

The tackier, the better. Guests should arrive wearing the most outrageous combination of Christmas and luau fashion imaginable. Think ugly Christmas sweaters paired with grass skirts, leis, and maybe a light-up Rudolph nose for good measure. Encourage accessories like oversized sunglasses, flashing Christmas lights necklaces, or fruit hats worthy of a Carmen Miranda comeback.

Decor Ideas:

Go all-in on mixing holiday cheer with luau decor. Hang tiki torches next to blinking reindeer lawn ornaments. Wrap Christmas lights around faux palm trees and create a "Tacky Tree" decorated with the most ridiculous, glittery ornaments you can find. Pineapples wearing Santa hats should make an appearance, naturally.

Food & Drinks:

Keep the food simple but fun with **Holiday Ham Sliders** (topped with pineapple slices) and a side of fruit salad served in hollowed-out watermelons. Create a Luau Punch station, where guests can pour their own colorful cocktails into tacky, holiday-themed drinkware. Think reindeer antler cups or coconut cups wearing Santa hats.

Party Activities:

- **Worst Outfit Contest**: It wouldn't be a tacky party without an award for the most outrageous ensemble. The winner of the "Worst Outfit" contest gets a lump of coal (don't worry, it's wrapped in glitter and tied with a bow for maximum flair).
- **Limbo with Christmas Lights**: Host a limbo contest under a pole wrapped in Christmas lights. Crank up some tropical holiday tunes, and watch as your guests compete to see who can bend the lowest in their mismatched, tacky outfits.

Pro Tips for Pulling Off an Unconventional Christmas Party

- **Tip 1: Lean Into the Theme** Go big or go home. These parties thrive on creativity, humor, and an unapologetic willingness to be silly. The more you commit, the more fun everyone will have.
- **Tip 2: Combine Music Styles** Curate a playlist that mixes classic Christmas carols with tropical beats. A reggae version of "Jingle Bells" is sure to get everyone in the spirit of the holidays—and the beach.
- **Tip 3: Have Fun with Party Favors** Send guests home with quirky favors like flip-flop-shaped Christmas ornaments, mini bottles of sunscreen with festive labels, or leis with jingle bells attached. Who says souvenirs are just for vacations?
- **Tip 4: Don't Forget the Photos** Set up a tropical-themed photo booth complete with props like inflatable flamingos, grass skirts, Santa hats, and oversized Christmas sunglasses. Encourage guests to strike their best beachy holiday pose and capture the hilarity.

* * *

No matter which theme you choose, your party is bound to be memorable. Feel free to mix and match elements from each idea, or let your imagination run wild and create something completely unique. The point of these unconventional parties is to have fun, break a few traditions, and give your guests an experience they'll never forget. After all, nothing says "Merry Misfits" like a holiday celebration no one saw coming!

Offbeat Christmas Games – Fun, Festive, and Ridiculously Entertaining

Let's be honest—holiday games can sometimes feel like an afterthought. There's the same ol' gift exchanges, charades, and maybe a round of trivia, but by the third Secret Santa party of the season, even the most die-hard Christmas fans start feeling a little "bah humbug." That's where this chapter comes in. It's time to throw in some unexpected, wildly creative, and laugh-out-loud funny games that will have your guests talking about your party until next Christmas.

If you're going to throw an unconventional Christmas party, you can't stop at just the decor and theme—your games need to match the energy. So put on your flamingo-patterned Santa hat and dive into a world where bowling involves coconuts, limbo comes with elf shoes, and balancing a pineapple on your head while hula dancing is completely normal.

READY? Let the games begin!

Santa's Flamingo Toss

Game Overview: Move over, cornhole! It's time to upgrade your lawn games with some tropical cheer. "Santa's Flamingo Toss" is the perfect mix of beachside fun and holiday magic, where you trade bean bags for Christmas ornaments and aim for the most iconic tropical bird of all—flamingos.

How to Play:

- Set up several plastic flamingo lawn ornaments in your yard (or indoors if you're feeling brave) and space them at different distances for varying levels of difficulty. You can find these beauties at most party supply stores.
- Provide your guests with Christmas ornaments (preferably plastic to avoid mid-game disasters) to toss onto the flamingos' necks. Each guest takes turns, aiming to hook their ornaments over the neck of the flamingo.

- Assign different point values based on the distance of each flamingo—closer ones might be worth fewer points, while the farthest flamingo could be the jackpot target.

Bonus Twist:

- Give each flamingo a holiday name—like "Flamingo Claus," "Jolly Beaks," or "Frosty the Flamingo"—and offer extra points for landing on specific ones. You could also create a "snowbird" flamingo decked out in tinsel and lights that offers double points for any successful toss!

Elf Limbo

Game Overview: What's better than limbo? Limbo with a festive twist, of course! "Elf Limbo" will test the flexibility of your guests, but this isn't your standard game. Imagine trying to bend backward while balancing in elf shoes, reindeer antlers, or maybe even a pair of oversized Christmas elf ears.

How to Play:

- Set up your limbo stick by wrapping a broom handle or curtain rod with Christmas lights or festive garland. Play some upbeat holiday tunes (tropical versions preferred!) to set the mood.
- Each player must limbo while wearing oversized elf shoes, which you can find online or at costume shops, or any silly holiday-themed footwear. If you really want to up the challenge, add reindeer antlers or jingly elf hats that throw off their balance.
- Start the limbo stick high and lower it after each successful round. As the limbo stick lowers, the game

becomes more challenging, and the sight of guests attempting to bend under the bar while jingling and wobbling will have everyone in stitches.

Bonus Twist:

- For an extra level of difficulty (and hilarity), make it a singing challenge: contestants must sing a Christmas carol while they limbo. Not only do they have to concentrate on bending low, but they'll need to keep their composure while belting out "Jingle Bells."

Christmas Coconut Bowling

Game Overview: Forget the bowling alley—this tropical Christmas game brings the lanes to you, but with a twist. Instead of bowling balls, players use coconuts. Instead of pins, you'll have stacks of festive, gift-wrapped boxes. Prepare for some wobbly strikes and unexpected gutter balls!

How to Play:

- Set up your bowling lane in the hallway, backyard, or living room, using gift-wrapped boxes as bowling pins. The bigger and flashier the wrapping, the better. Stack them in a traditional bowling pin formation (a triangle shape), but don't be afraid to add in extra decorations like tinsel or bows to make the pins feel truly festive.
- Each player takes turns rolling a coconut down the lane, aiming to knock down as many pins as possible. You can use painter's tape to mark a starting line on the floor.

- For added fun, give guests the chance to decorate their own coconuts with Christmas faces, turning them into characters like "Coconut Claus" or "Rudolph the Red-Nosed Coconut."

Bonus Twist:

- Throw in a few "special" pins wrapped in distinctive paper (like shiny gold or silver). If a player knocks down one of these pins, they win a bonus prize or an extra turn. Alternatively, make the game more challenging by placing a few "obstacle gifts" in the lane—boxes that players must avoid, or they'll lose points.

Snowball Toss

Game Overview: Just because you're ditching the cold doesn't mean you can't have a snowball fight—tropical style! "Snowball" Toss swaps real snowballs for soft, beach-inspired ones, letting players aim for oversized holiday-themed targets without the frostbite.

How to Play:

- Set up a series of large holiday-themed targets like oversized buckets, giant gift bags, or even stockings hung from the wall. Each target is assigned a different point value based on its size and distance.
- Use inflatable snowballs, plush toy balls, or lightweight beach balls as your "snowballs." Have players stand behind a designated throwing line and take turns tossing their snowballs into the targets.
- Score points based on where their snowballs land. The farther or smaller the target, the more points they earn.

Bonus Twist:

- Make each round progressively more difficult by adding silly throwing challenges, like tossing the snowball while spinning around, balancing on one foot, or wearing oversized oven mitts. This guarantees lots of laughs as your guests struggle to make the perfect throw.

Ho-Ho-Hula Dance-Off

Game Overview: Let's combine two things you never thought you'd see together: hula dancing and Santa hats. But wait, there's more. In this game, guests must hula dance *while* balancing a coconut or pineapple on their head. Think you've got the coordination to pull it off? Only one way to find out!

How to Play:

- Hand each participant a Santa hat and either a coconut or pineapple to balance on their head. To up the festive spirit, provide grass skirts and tropical leis.
- Crank up the holiday music (preferably some fun tropical versions of classic Christmas carols), and let the dance-off begin. Players must hula dance while keeping their balance and not dropping their fruit.
- The person who can keep dancing the longest without dropping their coconut or pineapple wins the contest!

Bonus Twist:

- Midway through the game, challenge participants to switch fruits or dance faster. Or, if you want to really raise the stakes, introduce a limbo round where they must continue balancing while attempting to duck under the limbo bar. The chaos and laughter are guaranteed.

Reindeer Ring Toss

Game Overview: Forget horseshoes—how about some reindeer antler ring toss? In this game, players wear inflatable reindeer antlers while others toss rings (or wreaths) to try and hook them on the antlers.

How to Play:

- One person wears a headband with inflatable reindeer antlers (available at party stores or online). The antler-wearer stands a few feet away while other guests take turns tossing rings at them.
- Use lightweight rings or DIY wreaths (you can make some using garland and wire), and challenge guests to see how many rings they can land on the antlers.
- Award points for each successful toss, and give bonus points for trick throws (under-the-leg, behind-the-back, etc.).

Bonus Twist:

- Make it a team game! Each team has an antler-wearer who can move their head and body to try to "catch" the rings, adding a bit of teamwork and strategy to the mix.

Holiday Piñata Smash

Game Overview: It's not just for birthdays—bring out the piñata for some holiday fun! This Christmas-themed piñata is filled with tropical goodies and Christmas treats. The challenge? Break it open without knocking over the inflatable palm trees nearby.

How to Play:

- Hang a festive piñata shaped like Santa, a reindeer, or a Christmas tree. Fill it with a mix of holiday candies, mini tropical toys (like tiny flamingos), and maybe even some Christmas crackers or novelty gifts.
- Blindfold each player, spin them around a few times, and let them swing at the piñata. The first person to break it open wins bragging rights (and everyone gets to enjoy the treats inside).
- If you're feeling extra festive, give the piñata a "tropical" twist by hanging it in a beach-themed area,

surrounded by inflatable decorations like palm trees and flamingos.

Bonus Twist:

- Instead of one big piñata, hide smaller piñatas around your party space and let guests hunt for them, smashing them open to reveal their surprise prizes.

Naughty or Nice Trivia

Game Overview: Test your guests' holiday knowledge with a trivia game that mixes traditional Christmas questions with some tropical fun. Do they know more about Santa's sleigh or Santa's tan?

How to Play:

- Divide guests into teams and alternate between asking Christmas trivia and tropical-themed questions. Mix it up with questions like "What's Santa's favorite reindeer?" and "Which fruit is the symbol of hospitality in Hawaii?"
- Score points for correct answers, but here's the twist: for every incorrect answer, a team member must perform a silly holiday dare, like singing "Jingle Bells" in a Hawaiian accent or wearing a ridiculous Christmas accessory for the rest of the game.

Bonus Twist:

- Throw in a "Naughty or Nice" round where players can choose between answering a trivia question or completing a funny holiday challenge.

Congratulations, you've now got a toolbox full of offbeat, tropical-inspired Christmas games that are guaranteed to bring your party to life. Whether you're tossing coconuts, balancing pineapples, or limbo-ing like an elf, these games are sure to create hilarious memories that your guests will be talking about for years to come.

The best part about these unconventional games? They're all about having fun, laughing until your sides hurt, and embracing the chaos of a Christmas party like no other. So get out there, deck those flamingos, and let the games begin!

Tropical-Inspired Christmas Treats – Sweet, Sunny, and Totally Delicious

Let's admit it: as much as we love traditional holiday treats, sometimes they can be a little too... heavy. Fruitcake that could double as a paperweight, cookies loaded with sugar and spice (but not so nice), and an endless supply of fudge that sticks to your ribs. This year, we're shaking things up by adding a little sunshine to your Christmas spread. Get ready for some tropical-inspired treats that will bring a burst of flavor, fun, and sunshine to your festivities. These light, refreshing, and vibrant dishes are guaranteed to brighten up even the snowiest winter day.

So put down that fruitcake (unless it's our revamped tropical version) and dive into a world where pineapples wear Santa hats, coconuts become snowballs, and nachos get a holiday makeover.

Grilled Pineapple Santa Skewers

Overview:

- Picture this: golden, caramelized pineapple slices, lightly grilled with cinnamon and sugar, and topped with whipped cream "snow." These festive skewers are the perfect blend of sweet and tropical, with a hint of holiday magic. They're easy to make, look impressive, and are sure to transport your guests to a beachside Christmas party.

How to Make It:

- Start by slicing fresh pineapples into rounds or chunks and thread them onto skewers.
- Grill the pineapple over medium heat until slightly charred and caramelized, then sprinkle with cinnamon and sugar as they cook for a holiday twist.
- After grilling, top each skewer with a generous dollop of whipped cream to create that "snowy" effect. The

contrast of the warm, grilled pineapple and cool whipped cream will keep your guests coming back for more.

Serving Tip:

- For an extra festive presentation, stick a mini Santa hat (use a strawberry for the red hat and a marshmallow for the fluffy white brim) on the top of each skewer. Lay the skewers on a bed of shredded coconut to give the appearance of snow on a tropical island.

Coconut Snowballs

Overview:

- Traditional snowballs are cold, but not these delightful coconut macaroons. Crispy on the outside, chewy on the inside, these treats are packed with coconut flavor and look like little snowballs that have rolled in from the tropics. They're the perfect snack for anyone who wants to enjoy the "snow" without the frostbite.

How to Make It:

- Mix shredded coconut with sweetened condensed milk and vanilla extract until it forms a thick, sticky mixture.
- Roll the mixture into small balls, place them on a baking sheet, and bake until golden brown on the outside but still chewy and moist on the inside.
- After baking, roll each macaroon in additional

shredded coconut or dust them with powdered sugar to give them that extra snowy appearance.

Serving Tip:

- For a fun, festive presentation, stack the coconut snowballs into a pyramid shape and add a mini star-shaped cookie at the top to create a snowball Christmas tree. These treats also pair perfectly with a tropical coconut-rum hot chocolate.

Christmas Nachos

Overview:

- Who says nachos are just for football games? Christmas nachos bring a festive, tropical twist to the snack table. With tortilla chips covered in melted cheese, red and green bell peppers, and a guacamole Christmas tree in the center, these nachos are the perfect savory dish to break up all the sweetness of the holiday spread. It's cheesy, colorful, and just plain fun.

How to Make It:

- Arrange a large platter of tortilla chips and sprinkle them with shredded cheese. Add red and green bell peppers for holiday color, and top with jalapeños for those who like a little heat.
- For the guacamole Christmas tree, shape a large dollop of guac into a tree form in the center of the nachos. Use queso fresco or sour cream to create snow, and

cherry tomatoes or pomegranate seeds as the ornaments.
- Place a star-shaped tortilla chip on top of the guacamole tree to complete the look.

Serving Tip:

- To really sell the festive theme, serve the nachos on a round platter so that the chips and guacamole form a wreath. You could even add sprigs of cilantro or parsley as "holly" to decorate the wreath.

Tropical Fruitcake

Overview:

- Ah, fruitcake. The infamous holiday treat that's often better used as a doorstop than dessert. But not anymore! This revamped tropical fruitcake uses vibrant tropical fruits like mango, papaya, kiwi, and pineapple, all soaked in rum, to create a version of fruitcake that's light, fruity, and actually delicious. It's boozy, it's bright, and it'll make you a fruitcake believer.

How to Make It:

- Start by chopping tropical fruits—mango, papaya, kiwi, pineapple—and soak them in dark rum overnight. This infuses the fruit with flavor and ensures the cake stays moist and packed with island spirit.
- Mix the soaked fruit with a light batter made from butter, sugar, eggs, and a dash of warm spices like

cinnamon and nutmeg. Bake until golden and fragrant, then brush the cake with more rum to keep it rich and flavorful.
- Let the cake cool completely before slicing, and for a festive finish, top it with a drizzle of rum glaze or powdered sugar.

Serving Tip:

- Garnish the cake with fresh slices of tropical fruit and edible flowers for a stunning presentation. You can even serve it alongside coconut ice cream or rum-infused whipped cream for the ultimate tropical holiday dessert.

Mango & Papaya Christmas Salsa

Overview:

- This salsa isn't your average holiday dip. Packed with fresh mango, papaya, lime, and a hint of chili, it brings a bright, zesty flavor to the table. It's the perfect accompaniment to your Christmas nachos, grilled meats, or even as a refreshing topping for your holiday feast.

How to Make It:

- Dice ripe mango, papaya, red onion, and jalapeño. Toss everything with fresh lime juice, cilantro, and a pinch of salt.
- For a festive twist, add pomegranate seeds or diced red bell pepper to give the salsa pops of holiday red.
- Chill for at least an hour before serving to let the flavors meld together.

Serving Tip:

- For a fun and tropical touch, serve the salsa in a hollowed-out pineapple or coconut shell. Pair it with tortilla chips, or use it as a topping for grilled shrimp or chicken skewers.

Key Lime Pie Christmas Bars

Overview:

- Want to lighten up your dessert table? These Key Lime Pie Christmas Bars are a zesty, tropical alternative to the heavier holiday desserts. Their tangy lime flavor will refresh your taste buds and add a pop of bright, citrusy goodness to your Christmas spread.

How to Make It:

- Start by making a graham cracker crust and baking it until golden. Meanwhile, mix key lime juice, sweetened condensed milk, and egg yolks for the filling.
- Pour the filling over the crust and bake until just set. Chill the bars for a few hours before slicing.
- Dust the bars with powdered sugar or drizzle with lime glaze for an extra festive finish.

Serving Tip:

- Garnish each bar with a small dollop of whipped cream and a slice of candied lime. Arrange the bars on a platter with sprigs of fresh mint for a simple, yet elegant holiday presentation.

Rum-Soaked Christmas Pudding

Overview:

- Inspired by the traditional British Christmas pudding, this tropical version replaces the heavy dried fruits with vibrant tropical varieties and a generous soak of rum. The result is a rich, fruity, and boozy dessert that will warm your heart—and your belly—on a chilly winter night.

How to Make It:

- Soak chopped tropical fruits like mango, pineapple, and papaya in dark rum overnight.
- Combine the fruit with a mixture of brown sugar, breadcrumbs, warm spices, and butter. Steam the pudding for several hours until firm and cooked through.
- Just before serving, drizzle with a rum-infused caramel sauce or a buttery rum glaze.

Serving Tip:

- For an impressive and dramatic presentation, light the pudding on fire! Carefully pour warmed rum over the pudding and ignite it just before serving. The flaming rum will delight your guests and add a little extra warmth to your tropical holiday celebration.

Christmas treats don't have to be the same every year. By adding tropical flavors and a playful twist, you can surprise your guests with delicious, light, and vibrant dishes that bring a little island magic to your holiday feast. Whether you're grilling pineapple skewers, enjoying coconut snowballs, or revamping fruitcake with rum-soaked tropical fruits, these recipes will transport everyone to a sunny beach, even if it's snowing outside.

So, get ready to bring the heat to your Christmas table—tropical style!

Fun Twists on Holiday Traditions – Redefining the Christmas Spirit

We all love holiday traditions, right? Whether it's Secret Santa, singing carols, or watching *Home Alone* for the 75th time, these little rituals make the season feel magical. But let's be honest—sometimes it's nice to break the mold. What if we could take those cherished traditions and add a tropical twist? Imagine exchanging quirky beach-themed gifts, singing *Jingle Bells* to a reggae beat, or balancing on a surfboard (indoors!) while wearing reindeer antlers.

In this chapter, we're giving your favorite holiday traditions a sun-soaked upgrade. You don't need to head to the tropics for a Christmas like no other—these ideas will bring the beach vibes straight to your living room, and with them, a healthy dose of laughter and unforgettable fun. So let's dive into how you can give your holiday classics a makeover, tropical style.

Tropical Secret Santa

Overview: Secret Santa is always a hit at holiday parties, but this time, we're trading in the generic gifts for something a little more fun—tropical-themed presents! From pineapple-shaped mugs to beach towels with Santa on a surfboard, this Secret Santa will have your guests dreaming of a sunny holiday, even if it's snowing outside.

How to Play:

- Start by setting the ground rules like any traditional Secret Santa game, where everyone draws a name and keeps their recipient a secret. But here's the twist: all gifts must be tropical-themed. Encourage your guests to get creative, thinking outside the Christmas box with beachy and sunny gift ideas.
- The more quirky and playful, the better! Think items that bring the tropics to Christmas, like a flamingo-shaped wine bottle holder, or flip-flop ornaments decked out in tiny Christmas lights.

Gift Ideas:

- Pineapple-shaped mugs or tumblers.
- Beach towels with holiday or tropical designs.
- Flip-flop-shaped Christmas ornaments.
- Tiki bar accessories like cocktail stirrers or mini umbrellas.
- Coconut-scented candles or bath products that smell like a beach day in December.

Bonus Twist:

- Once the gifts are exchanged, have everyone guess who their Secret Santa was. If the guess is wrong, the recipient has to perform a silly task, like wearing a tropical accessory (leis, sunglasses, or a straw hat) for the rest of the party.

Christmas Karaoke – Island Style

Overview: Everyone loves a good Christmas karaoke session, but why not spice things up with a little island rhythm? This twist on the classic karaoke game swaps traditional tunes for holiday favorites with a tropical beat. Think reggae versions of *Jingle Bells* or a steel drum cover of *Silent Night*. For those brave enough, challenge them to rewrite the lyrics with beach or surfing references for extra fun!

How to Play:

- Set up a karaoke machine (or use a karaoke app) with a selection of holiday classics. But here's where the magic happens: add a tropical beat to those songs! You can find reggae, calypso, or even Hawaiian versions of Christmas carols online or simply use a steel drum backing track.
- For the truly creative, encourage guests to rewrite the lyrics to reflect a sunny Christmas. Imagine *Frosty the*

Snowman turning into *Sunny the Sandman*, or *Deck the Halls* becoming *Deck the Palms*.

Example Lyric Reworks:

- "Dashing through the sand, on a one-flip-flop sleigh…"
- "Walking in an island wonderland…"
- "We wish you a sunny Christmas, and a beachy New Year…"

Bonus Twist:

- Make it a competition! Create scorecards for creativity, performance, and how well they capture the tropical theme. The winner gets a tropical prize, like a ukulele or a fun cocktail set, and of course, endless bragging rights.

Rudolph's Surfing Challenge

Overview: It's time to take Rudolph out of the snow and onto the waves! This hilarious team-building game involves balancing on an inflatable surfboard while wearing reindeer antlers. It's a test of balance, skill, and who can hold their giggles the longest before wiping out. The catch? The first one to fall has to sing a Christmas carol solo!

How to Play:

- Set up an inflatable surfboard indoors or on a flat, safe surface. Players take turns hopping on and trying to balance while wearing reindeer antlers.
- The goal is to stay balanced for as long as possible. Once someone falls off, they must sing a Christmas carol for the group. If they want to escape embarrassment, they can attempt to sing the carol with a tropical twist—like turning *Jingle Bells* into *Jingle Shells*.

Game Tips:

- Make sure the space around the surfboard is clear to prevent accidents (and make room for all the laughter).
- To make the game even more fun, have contestants dress in festive beachwear or Santa-themed swim gear.

Bonus Twist:

- For extra chaos and fun, make it a relay race! Split the guests into teams, and each member has to balance on the board for a set time before switching to the next teammate. If someone falls, the whole team must sing a Christmas carol together—maybe a reggae version of *Deck the Halls*?

Island Gift Wrapping Contest

Overview: Gift wrapping is a holiday staple, but who says it has to be all bows and ribbons? In this Island Gift Wrapping Contest, guests are challenged to wrap their presents using tropical materials like palm leaves, seashells, and bright beachy colors. It's a race to see who can create the most eye-catching and festive tropical package!

How to Play:

- Set up a gift-wrapping station with tropical materials such as raffia ribbons, palm leaves, bright tropical-patterned wrapping paper, faux flowers, and seashells.
- Each player has a set amount of time to wrap a gift using only the tropical materials provided. They can get as creative as they want, but the goal is to make their gift look as festive and beachy as possible.
- When time's up, a panel of judges (or the whole group) scores each wrapped gift on creativity, style, and how well they embraced the tropical theme.

Bonus Twist:

- Add a challenge! For instance, require players to wrap their gift while wearing oversized beach gloves or give them only five minutes to complete the task. It's all about adding a little pressure (and lots of laughs).

Beach Blanket Christmas Movie Marathon

Overview: Cozy Christmas movie nights are great, but why not trade in the fireplace for a beach blanket? A Beach Blanket Christmas Movie Marathon invites your guests to kick back on beach towels, sip tropical drinks, and watch holiday classics with a summery twist.

How to Set It Up:

- Lay out beach towels, beach chairs, and inflatable pool floats around your living room or outdoor space. Use a projector or TV to screen classic Christmas movies.
- Serve tropical snacks and drinks to keep the island vibe going, like piña coladas, coconut popcorn, and fruit platters with pineapple and mango.

Movie Ideas:

- Classic Christmas movies like *Elf*, *Home Alone*, and *The Grinch*. Bonus points if you create your own tropical drinking game or turn it into a "beach pajama" contest to see who shows up in the most festive, summery sleepwear.

Bonus Twist:

- Encourage everyone to vote on their favorite movie of the night, and whoever's pick wins gets a special beachy prize, like a pineapple-shaped cocktail shaker or a surfboard-shaped cheese board.

Traditions are great, but when you add a little sunshine and creativity, they become unforgettable. Whether you're swapping tropical gifts in Secret Santa, balancing on a surfboard in reindeer antlers, or belting out Christmas carols with a reggae beat, these fun twists on holiday traditions are guaranteed to make your celebrations stand out.

By mixing up the old with the new, you'll give your guests a holiday experience that's full of laughter, surprises, and a little island magic. So go ahead, give these tropical twists a try and watch your Christmas party become the event of the season—one that everyone will be talking about until next year.

Humorous Holiday Disasters – What Could Go Wrong?

Ah, the holidays—a time for laughter, joy, and... *catastrophic chaos*. Let's be real, no Christmas celebration is complete without something going hilariously off the rails. You can plan all you want, but once Aunt Carol gets into the eggnog, or someone plugs in one too many string lights, things are bound to go sideways. Add in a tropical theme, and you've got a recipe for some seriously comical calamities.

This chapter is a collection of holiday mishaps so ridiculous, they could only happen at a tropical Christmas party. From inflatable Santas that take flight to palm trees that burst into flames, we're diving into the epic disasters that will make you laugh, cringe, and maybe rethink that 12-foot blow-up snowman. So, grab your margarita, sit back, and enjoy these tales of tropical Christmas parties gone wrong. And remember: these aren't just cautionary tales—they're survival guides.

The Palm Tree Tipping Incident

Overview: Imagine this: you've swapped out the classic pine tree for a beautiful, real palm tree, decked out in lights and ornaments. It's the centerpiece of your tropical Christmas party. What could go wrong? Well, turns out, *a lot*. Welcome to the "Palm Tree Tipping Incident."

The Story: Everything was going great. The guests were sipping their piña coladas, the music was playing, and your palm tree was shining brightly in the corner of the room. But then it started to wobble. Maybe it was the weight of the 5 pounds of Christmas lights you wrapped around it, or maybe it was the tequila-spiked eggnog, but that tree was *leaning*. Before you know it, your beautiful tropical Christmas centerpiece tipped over like a drunk at the office holiday party, right into the punch bowl.

Cue the chaos. Guests screamed, diving out of the way as your palm tree gracefully collapsed, sending flamingo ornaments flying and drenching everyone in "Merry Margaritas." The punch splattered across the floor, taking down a tray of coconut shrimp in its path, while your inflatable Santa looked on, judging your life choices.

And then, to top it all off, the tree tangled itself in your fairy lights, turning your living room into an electric hazard. One guest heroically rushed to unplug the lights while another attempted to prop the tree back up—using a flamingo lawn ornament as a support. It didn't work, but the photos will live in infamy.

Lesson Learned: Maybe don't wrap your palm tree like it's Times Square on New Year's Eve. And if you do, make sure there's a clear escape route when the inevitable tree collapse happens.

The Inflatable Santa Blowout

Overview: In the world of tropical Christmas decorations, inflatable Santas are a must. Who wouldn't want a jolly St. Nick chilling on a surfboard in their front yard, right? But if you've ever wondered what happens when you push those inflatables a bit too far, let me introduce you to the epic "Inflatable Santa Blowout."

The Story: Meet Dave. Dave thought he could take his tropical Christmas décor to the next level with an inflatable Santa—complete with sunglasses, a Hawaiian shirt, and a surfboard. But here's the thing about inflatables: they don't come with instructions on *how much air is too much air*. Dave, being a "more is better" kind of guy, decided to pump up Santa until he was practically bursting at the seams. Santa looked magnificent... for about 10 minutes.

As guests arrived, they marveled at the towering figure of Santa the Surfer Dude. But soon enough, you could hear the faintest hissing sound. Was it the wind? Nope. Santa was slowly inflating beyond his limit, like a balloon at a kid's birthday party—only this time, the stakes were higher. Then came the big moment: with a thunderous *pop*, Santa exploded.

Yes, you read that right. Santa. Exploded. Pieces of nylon went flying across the yard, Rudolph lost his nose in the blast, and poor Mrs. Claus took a direct hit from Santa's disembodied arm. The party froze in stunned silence for about three seconds before bursting into uncontrollable laughter as bits of inflatable Santa rained down like confetti.

Lesson Learned: When the package says "do not overinflate," believe them. And maybe avoid positioning your inflatable Santa directly under power lines—you know, just in case.

Escape the Heat – Surviving a Christmas Heatwave

Overview: We all dream of escaping the cold during the holidays, but what happens when your tropical Christmas theme becomes *too* realistic? Enter: "The Christmas Heatwave," where your festive luau turns into a sweat-drenched survival game.

The Story: You've decked out your space with tiki torches, Hawaiian shirts, and a beautiful coconut centerpiece. Guests are wearing their festive leis, and you've cranked up the heater to create that "authentic tropical atmosphere." But then something happens. The temperature *keeps rising*. You thought it would be fun to pretend it was summer in December—until it actually felt like summer in December.

It starts small. Someone makes a joke about it being "hotter than Rudolph's nose," and everyone laughs. But then the ice in the drinks melts almost immediately. The air starts to feel thick and heavy. Sweat beads form on your guests' foreheads as they fan themselves with their napkins. Your coconut drinks are starting to resemble lukewarm puddles of regret, and the Christmas ham? Let's just say it's entered the realm of *over*-roasted.

People are trying to remain festive, but you notice one guest sneak outside to cool off while another is using the inflatable palm tree as a makeshift fan. And just when you think it can't get worse, the inflatable reindeer you bought start to deflate, not from lack of air, but from sheer exhaustion in the heat.

At this point, your once-jolly crowd is now a sluggish, sweaty mess, and the grand finale? Someone tries to take a photo with a Santa hat—only to remove it seconds later, dripping with sweat, the white fluff stuck to their head like a wet mop.

Lesson Learned: Keep the tropical Christmas vibe under control—there's a difference between "fun in the sun" and "Christmas in a sauna." And never underestimate the power of air conditioning. Or, you know, *any* kind of cooling system.

The Sand-in-the-Socks Debacle

The Sand-in-the-Socks Debacle

Overview: Ah, sand—the hallmark of any great beach experience. But when you bring it inside for a tropical Christmas party? It quickly turns from fun décor to a gritty disaster. Welcome to the "Sand-in-the-Socks Debacle."

The Story: Someone, in their infinite wisdom, thought it would be a fantastic idea to spread sand across the living room floor to give the party that "authentic beach vibe." You step inside and feel the satisfying crunch of sand between your toes—Christmas on the beach, right? But soon, things start to go wrong.

It begins with the shoes. People kick them off, only to realize they're full of sand. Socks? Sand. Somehow, even *pockets* start filling with sand. You notice that the sand, which started off as a cute decorative element, is now tracking all over the house. It's in the kitchen, in the bathroom, and—*oh no*—on the gifts.

Then comes the ultimate disaster: someone spills their drink. What was once a light dusting of beachy sand is now a sticky, slushy mess. People are slipping, sliding, and cursing as they try to navigate what's become a mini tropical mudslide in your living room. And don't even ask about the cleanup—sand may be fun on the beach, but it's a nightmare in your vacuum cleaner.

Lesson Learned: If you feel the urge to bring the beach inside, maybe stick to *seashells* and *decorative nets*. Sand belongs outdoors, and nowhere near your living room, unless you want to be cleaning it up until next Christmas.

Christmas isn't Christmas without a little disaster, and tropical-themed parties seem to invite chaos of the most hilarious kind. Whether it's an exploding Santa, a palm tree catastrophe, or a heatwave that turns your living room into a sauna, these stories remind us that even the best-laid holiday plans can go comically wrong.

But here's the thing—those mishaps are what make your party memorable. So, the next time your inflatable reindeer goes rogue, or you find sand in places sand should *never* be, remember: it's all part of the adventure. After all, it's not a true Christmas party without a few laughs, a little chaos, and maybe a palm tree on fire.

Gifts No One Wants (But Everyone Will Laugh About)

We've all been there—sitting in a circle, watching someone unwrap their gift with anticipation, only to see their face fall as they realize they've just received another set of socks or a candle that smells like "Winter Snow." But what if we told you that gifts don't have to be *wanted* to be a hit? In fact, the best gifts are often the ones no one asked for but will never forget.

This chapter is dedicated to those hilariously useless, utterly impractical tropical-themed gifts that will leave your guests laughing long after the party is over. These gifts may not spark joy in the traditional sense, but they'll definitely spark a lot of laughter—and isn't that what the holiday spirit is all about?

A Box of Sand

Overview: Nothing screams "tropical getaway" like... a box of sand. That's right, it's the gift that quite literally gives you a taste of the beach without the actual fun part of being there. "A Box of Beach" is exactly what it sounds like—a box filled with sand and the promise of imaginary island adventures. Bonus points for delivering this with a completely straight face, as if this is the most luxurious gift in the world.

How It Plays Out: Picture this: your friend or colleague tears into their beautifully wrapped gift, expecting something exciting, only to find a box filled with... sand. Maybe you attach a cheeky note that says, "Your tropical vacation awaits! Just add water and pretend you're on an exotic island." As they stare at the sand in confusion, everyone else is howling with laughter.

And the best part? The clean-up. They'll be finding bits of sand in their living room carpet for months—an ever-present reminder of your hilariously misguided generosity.

Why It's Funny: This is the ultimate anti-gift: it's not useful, it's not particularly exciting, and it's definitely not something anyone asked for. But that's what makes it so funny. It's absurd, it's unexpected, and it's bound to be the gift everyone talks about for years to come.

The Inflatable Reindeer for the Lawn

Overview: Inflatable lawn decorations are a holiday staple, but nothing sets the tone for a tropical Christmas quite like an inflatable reindeer wearing sunglasses, lying on a beach towel. It sounds festive, right? Well, until you realize that inflatable decorations have a tendency to deflate when you least expect it. Say hello to the "Inflatable Reindeer Blowout."

How It Plays Out: You hand over the box with pride, describing the inflatable reindeer as the perfect addition to anyone's holiday décor. They set it up on the lawn, confident that they now have the most Instagram-worthy Christmas display in the neighborhood. For the first hour or two, it's all smiles and compliments as Santa's reindeer lounges under a string of tropical Christmas lights.

But then, halfway through the evening, something happens. The air slowly escapes, and Rudolph starts to sag. By midnight, the once-proud reindeer is sprawled flat on the lawn, looking more like a beach accident than a Christmas icon. Guests point and laugh, and the homeowner is left with a deflated mess that looks like reindeer roadkill.

Why It's Funny: There's something inherently hilarious about inflatable decorations that collapse in on themselves. It's the slow, inevitable downfall of a once-mighty reindeer, and the fact that it happens during the party only adds to the fun. Plus, the visual of a reindeer lying flat, looking like it needs a nap more than a sleigh ride, is pure comedy.

Pineapple-Scented Candles

Overview: At first glance, a pineapple-scented candle seems like the perfect tropical gift. It's fun, fruity, and reminds you of sipping piña coladas on a beach. But what no one tells you is that once you light it, the overpowering smell will make your home feel like a piña colada factory exploded—and it'll stick around for *days*.

How It Plays Out: You give your friend the candle with a smile, saying, "This will make your whole house smell like a tropical paradise!" They thank you and light it that evening, excited to embrace the beach vibes. But as the hours pass, the scent intensifies. The house now reeks of sugary pineapple sweetness so strong that even opening the windows doesn't help. By day two, their home smells like someone dumped a blender full of piña coladas everywhere. It's a scent they can't escape, even when they blow the candle out.

Why It's Funny: The sheer over-the-top nature of the scent makes this gift a gag in itself. What starts as a pleasant aroma quickly becomes an overpowering, inescapable tropical nightmare. And as much as the recipient may try to laugh it off, they'll be living in the world's strongest piña colada for days. It's the gift that keeps on giving—whether they want it or not.

Tropical Christmas Sweaters

Overview: Ugly Christmas sweaters have become a holiday tradition, but this tropical twist takes it to the next level. Imagine a sweater featuring Santa on a surfboard, palm trees strung with lights, and reindeer in sunglasses. It's not just ugly—it's aggressively tacky, and absolutely impossible to wear in public without turning heads for all the wrong reasons.

How It Plays Out: You hand over the sweater with a straight face, and your friend opens it to reveal a blindingly bright pattern of neon palm trees and surfing reindeer. They try to smile as they slip it on, only to realize they now look like they're attending the world's worst Christmas luau. The real hilarity kicks in when they realize they're expected to wear this monstrosity for the rest of the party—and possibly to their next holiday event.

Why It's Funny: The combination of clashing holiday themes (snowmen in Hawaiian shirts? Sure, why not!) makes this sweater so bad, it's good. Plus, it's a guaranteed conversation starter—and who doesn't love a gift that brings everyone together for a good laugh?

Miniature Desktop Palm Tree

Overview: Ever wish you could bring a little piece of the beach to the office? Well, with the Miniature Desktop Palm Tree, now you can... sort of. This tiny plastic palm tree is the perfect "decoration" for those who dream of working from a tropical island, but in reality, it's just a dust-collecting eyesore.

How It Plays Out: Your friend unwraps the gift and sees a plastic palm tree, complete with fake coconuts and a sunbathing Santa figurine. They awkwardly thank you, unsure of where to even place this tiny disaster. It spends the next few days on their desk, confusing coworkers and collecting dust, until they finally find an excuse to "accidentally" knock it over into the trash.

Why It's Funny: It's funny because it's completely pointless. A plastic palm tree in the dead of winter feels out of place in the best way possible, and the recipient's struggle to find a use for it makes it even more hilarious.

Beach Ball Snow Globe

Overview: Snow globes are classic Christmas décor, but why not swap the snow for sand? The Beach Ball Snow Globe takes a traditional holiday decoration and flips it on its head. Instead of snowflakes, you have tiny beach balls, palm trees, and seashells swirling around when you shake it.

How It Plays Out: Your friend opens the box, expecting a festive snow globe, only to find a beach scene inside. Instead of snowflakes, they watch as tiny palm trees and beach umbrellas spin around inside the globe. They shake it a few times, laughing at the absurdity of a snow globe that's entirely snow-free. The next dilemma? Where exactly does one display a sand globe during the holidays?

Why It's Funny: It's a snow globe without the snow, which makes it the perfect tropical gag gift. The irony of having a "Christmas decoration" that celebrates the beach is too funny to pass up.

A Bottle of "Ocean Breeze" (aka Air)

Overview: For the minimalist prankster, there's no better gift than a bottle labeled "Ocean Breeze" that's literally just filled with air. Yep—this is the gift that promises a fresh beach breeze but delivers absolutely nothing. It's a hilarious non-gift that will leave the recipient scratching their head in confusion.

How It Plays Out: Your friend eagerly unwraps their beautifully packaged gift to find a glass bottle labeled "Ocean Breeze." Intrigued, they open it, expecting a refreshing scent, but they're met with… nothing. The gift is literally just a bottle of air. As everyone else laughs, the recipient tries to play along, but it's clear they're still wondering, "Is this it?"

Why It's Funny: It's the ultimate prank gift because it's so pointless. The sheer absurdity of gifting someone nothing but air, dressed up as something special, is guaranteed to get a laugh. Plus, it's an eco-friendly gift, right?

* * *

Not every gift has to be practical—or even wanted—to be memorable. These tropical-themed gag gifts may be completely useless, but they're guaranteed to bring a smile (and maybe a groan) to your holiday festivities. Whether it's a box of sand, an exploding reindeer, or a candle that smells like a never-ending piña colada, these presents will keep

Santa's Outrageous Outfits – Dressing the Jolly Old Elf for the Tropics

Forget the traditional red suit and fur-trimmed hat—Santa's about to take a much-needed vacation to the tropics! In this chapter, we'll dive into some hilariously over-the-top tropical makeovers for Santa and his merry crew. Think Hawaiian shirts, reindeer in sunglasses, and even Frosty the Snowman hitting the surf. These outfit ideas will add a lighthearted, whimsical twist to any tropical-themed Christmas celebration, ensuring even the most iconic holiday figure looks beach-ready.

Santa Claus in a Hawaiian Shirt

Santa's been in the North Pole for centuries, and it's time for a change of scenery. Picture this: instead of his heavy red suit, Santa steps off the sleigh wearing a breezy Hawaiian shirt, perfectly capturing the laid-back beach vibe.

How to Style It:

Top: Forget the wooly coat. Santa's now sporting a bright Hawaiian shirt adorned with vibrant palm trees, hibiscus flowers, and maybe even a flamingo or two. The louder, the better!

Bottom: His usual trousers are swapped for festive Bermuda shorts. They can be candy cane-striped or boldly green, bringing just the right amount of Christmas flair to his beachside retreat.

Footwear: Those chunky black boots? Not in this heat! Santa now strolls in flip-flops, holiday-themed, of course, with mini Santas or reindeer on the straps.

Accessories: To really seal the deal, Santa's sporting a lei around his neck and a wide-brimmed straw hat in place of his classic fur-trimmed one. Don't forget the oversized sunglasses that

Santa definitely needs to shield his eyes from the glaring tropical sun.

Why It's Funny:

Seeing Santa ditch his traditional look and embrace the beach life is pure comedy gold. The image of him wearing a Hawaiian shirt with a margarita in hand, toes in the sand, is a hilarious juxtaposition to his usual chilly North Pole vibe. You can almost hear him saying "Mele Kalikimaka" as he slides into full vacation mode.

Reindeer with Sunglasses

Santa's not the only one getting a tropical makeover—his reindeer are swapping sleigh bells for sunblock in this heat! Dasher, Dancer, and the rest of the crew are looking more like beach bums than sleigh-pullers.

How to Style It:

Antlers: Deck out those iconic antlers with tiny, blinking Christmas lights or mini leis, bringing some festive tropical fun to their otherwise wintery look.

Sunglasses: Every reindeer needs a pair of cool, oversized shades. Think neon colors or novelty glasses shaped like pineapples or flamingos to really lean into the vacation aesthetic.

Accessories: For the final touch, drape each reindeer in a sarong or lightweight beach towel, and throw a beach ball or surfboard into the mix. If you're working with real-life pets, they'll look even more ridiculous—cue endless laughs! (Just no actual sunblock on them, unless they're humans.)

Why It's Funny:

Nothing says Christmas hilarity like a majestic reindeer looking ready for a poolside lounge, rather than navigating a snowstorm. Slap on those shades and suddenly Rudolph goes from sleigh leader to surf instructor in one absurd transformation.

Santa's Lifeguard Look

What's more reassuring than Santa? Santa as your beach lifeguard, of course! He's swapping the sleigh for a lifeguard chair, complete with his iconic red, but in lifeguard-approved swimwear.

How to Style It:

Top: A bright red tank top or sleeveless tee with "Santa Lifeguard" printed on the front, letting everyone know he's not just about delivering gifts—he's also saving swimmers from drowning in holiday eggnog.

Bottom: Red swim trunks, still on-brand, of course. They come with white candy cane stripes down the side for that extra festive touch.

Footwear: Santa's rocking the classic white flip-flops, or even water shoes, to complete the lifeguard-on-duty vibe.

Accessories: A whistle dangles around his neck, ready to blow if someone's caught being *too* jolly. His Santa hat gets an upgrade with a mesh back, and of course, he's holding a red lifeguard float decorated with tinsel.

Why It's Funny:

The sight of Santa blowing a whistle from a lifeguard chair, scanning the horizon for stray beach balls instead of naughty kids, is too much to handle. It's a far cry from guiding his reindeer, but let's be honest—he looks right at home.

Mrs. Claus Goes to the Beach

Move over, Santa—Mrs. Claus is here to show you how to truly enjoy a tropical holiday. She's leaving behind her apron and cookie sheets in favor of palm trees and piña coladas.

How to Style It:
Outfit: A floral muumuu or a bright sundress replaces her traditional winter dress. In holiday spirit, of course, it comes in bold reds and greens, decked with hibiscus flowers.

Footwear: Mrs. Claus opts for stylish wedge sandals or comfy flip-flops, embellished with a tiny holly sprig for some extra holiday flair.

Accessories: A wide-brimmed straw sunhat with a giant red bow, oversized sunglasses, and a coconut drink in hand. She might even carry a Christmas-themed beach bag packed with "sunblock" and tinsel-wrapped towels.

Why It's Funny:
Mrs. Claus, typically seen baking cookies and keeping things

cozy in the North Pole, is now transformed into a sun-loving beach goddess. Picture her sipping a drink out of a coconut while asking Santa if he remembered the sunscreen. It's a perfect and unexpected twist on her usual role.

Elf on Vacation

The elves are also getting in on the action! After a busy holiday season, they deserve some relaxation too. Think miniature board shorts and tiny coconut drinks—these elves are officially on island time.

How to Style It:

Outfit: Tiny board shorts and Hawaiian shirts in festive colors make these hardworking elves look ready for a beach volleyball match. Add a tiny Santa hat with a tropical print twist to complete the look.

Footwear: Whether they're wearing mini flip-flops or going barefoot, these elves are fully embracing the sand between their toes.

Accessories: Tiny surfboards, inflatable pool floaties, or even a mini margarita in hand for that true vacation feel.

Why It's Funny:

The thought of the diligent elves, usually busy in Santa's workshop, lounging on the beach with their feet up is comedy perfection. Throw in a few beach umbrellas and some elf-sized piña coladas, and you've got a scene that's too good not to laugh at.

Frosty the Surfer Snowman

Sure, Frosty might melt in the tropics, but that won't stop him from catching a few waves first! This version of Frosty is swapping snowdrifts for surfboards.

How to Style It:

Outfit: A Hawaiian shirt draped over his snowman body, a straw hat perched on his head, and sunglasses on his icy nose.

Accessories: A surfboard tucked under one branch-arm and a tropical drink in the other, Frosty is ready to hang ten. You can even surround him with seashells and sand to complete the tropical snowman vibe.

Why It's Funny:

Frosty lounging on a beach instead of freezing in a snowstorm is about as absurd as it gets. Throw in a sunblock bottle by his side (though we all know it's futile), and you've got the ultimate beachside comedy.

Reindeer Lifeguard Team

Santa's reindeer are no longer just pulling sleighs—they've leveled up to become a full-fledged lifeguard team.

How to Style It:

Outfit: Lifeguard trunks in red, of course, and whistles around their necks. Each reindeer gets their own rescue float, and they're all sporting festive sunglasses and holiday Santa hats with tropical flair.

Accessories: Pose them next to a kiddie pool or inflatable water toys for that perfect beach lifeguard aesthetic.

Why It's Funny:

The image of reindeer sitting in lifeguard chairs, keeping a watchful eye over the festivities, is peak comedy. Instead of guiding Santa's sleigh, they're making sure everyone is safe from beach-related "accidents".

* * *

Santa and his crew have worked hard all year, so why not give them a tropical vacation? From Santa in a Hawaiian shirt to Mrs. Claus sipping coconut water, these outfit ideas bring a fun, sun-soaked twist to Christmas. Whether you're dressing up yourself, your pets, or even your decorations, these tropical versions of the North Pole gang will keep everyone laughing and bring a whole new level of whimsy to your holiday celebration. After all, even the jolliest holiday characters deserve a beach break!

The Aftermath – Cleaning up After the Tropic Christmas

Every great party comes with an inevitable next step: the dreaded cleanup. After throwing your wild tropical Christmas bash, your living room may look like it hosted both a luau and a hurricane. Sand in the carpet, pineapple leftovers taking over the fridge, and deflated decorations that are clinging to life. But don't fret—in this final chapter, we'll walk through the hilarious trials of post-party cleanup. With humor, grit, and maybe a cocktail (because let's be honest, you'll need one), we'll help you face the chaos left in the wake of your beachside Christmas.

How to Remove Sand from Your Living Room

Overview:

That bucket of sand you so enthusiastically dumped onto your living room floor last night for the "authentic beach vibe"? Well, it's now your sworn enemy. Welcome to your new reality: an endless battle with grains of sand that seem to multiply by the minute. It's like the universe decided your living room should permanently resemble a tropical wasteland.

What You'll Need:

- **Vacuum Cleaner:** Preferably one that's up for a serious challenge, like sucking up all the regrets from last night.
- **Rake:** Why not? If there's enough sand, your living room might as well be a zen garden.
- **Fans:** Use these strategically to blow sand into your neighbor's yard, because sharing is caring.

Step-by-Step:

How to Remove Sand from Your Living Room

1. **Start with Denial:** Sit on your couch (which is also now full of sand) and contemplate leaving the beachy mess right where it is. Who *doesn't* love a permanent tropical vibe in their house?
2. **Get Real:** Realize this sand will eventually find its way into your bed, your laundry, and somehow your toothbrush. Time to accept your fate and grab the vacuum.
3. **Strategic Vacuuming:** Sand has the magical ability to sneak into places you didn't know existed. Use every vacuum attachment known to mankind, even the weird ones. You'll need them.
4. **Consider Relocation:** After the 47th pass of the vacuum and still finding sand, begin browsing for actual beach homes. They already have sand everywhere—problem solved!

Why It's Funny:

Trying to remove sand from a place it never belonged is like trying to scoop up the ocean with a teaspoon. The absurdity of vacuuming your life away makes it prime for comic relief, especially when it feels like you're starring in your own personal episode of *Survivor*.

Dealing with Too Much Pineapple

Overview:

Your "tropical Christmas" theme seemed like the perfect excuse to go heavy on the pineapple—so much so that you might have bought out the entire produce section. Now, you're faced with a fridge overflowing with pineapple chunks, slices, and questionable pineapple-shaped party favors. What do you do with the excess? Let's get creative.

Creative Uses for Leftover Pineapple:

- **Smoothies:** Dump all that pineapple into a blender, add coconut milk, and pretend you're still at the party. Bonus: you can drink your frustration away in smoothie form.
- **Pizza Toppings:** Instigate the ultimate pineapple-on-pizza debate by topping *every* meal with pineapple for the next week. Your friends will either love you or unfriend you.

Dealing with Too Much Pineapple

- **Pineapple Salsa:** Mix those pineapple chunks with some red onion, cilantro, and lime for a fresh salsa. You'll have tropical-flavored nachos until the end of time.
- **Re-Gifting:** Who wouldn't want a pineapple as a Christmas gift? Wrap it up, throw on a bow, and you've got yourself a quirky last-minute present for the coworker you forgot.
- **Pineapple Punch:** Grab that leftover rum and make a punch. In no time, no one will care about the mess anymore (or even remember it).

Why It's Funny:

Having so much pineapple that you have to find increasingly ridiculous ways to use it turns the fruit into an ongoing joke. By the end, you'll be convinced that pineapple is taking over your life —or your fridge, at the very least.

Tackling the Tiki Torch Disaster

Overview:

Tiki torches were *such* a great idea for your outdoor (or indoor, if you got overly enthusiastic) tropical party. Fast forward to the morning after, and now you're dealing with spilled fuel, broken torches, and that lingering smoky smell that won't go away no matter how many candles you light. Time to extinguish more than just the flames.

How to Clean Up:

1. **Avoidance:** Stare at the tiki torches and consider just leaving them there forever. Tell yourself it's "permanent ambiance," even though it smells more like "arson chic."
2. **Extinguish the Evidence:** If they're still standing (or if someone hasn't knocked them over yet), carefully take them down. Try not to singe anything important in the process.

3. **Torch Disposal:** What do you do with half-burned torches? Is there a place where rejected tiki torches go to retire? Debate storing them for next year, knowing full well you're never hosting again.
4. **Fuel Spill SOS:** If you've spilled fuel on your patio or, worse, your carpet, it's time for some serious scrubbing. Or just throw a beach towel over it and call it "tropical flair."

Why It's Funny:

Tiki torches always seem like a fantastic idea until they're dripping fuel or looking like sad, charred remnants of a good time. The clean-up struggle brings out the full absurdity of these flaming sticks of regret.

Deflating Santa and His Reindeer

Overview:

Last night, your inflatable Santa and reindeer were the stars of the show, but this morning? Santa's slumped over, and his reindeer are looking deflated—both figuratively and literally. The time has come to bid farewell to your jolly inflatable friends.

Step-by-Step Guide to Deflation:

1. **Face the Truth:** Take a long look at Santa, now looking like he partied harder than anyone. It's a bit sad, but also a bit hilarious—he definitely peaked.
2. **Deflation Party:** Slowly deflate each inflatable, savoring the sound of the air escaping along with your hopes of ever fitting them back in the box they came in.
3. **Roll 'Em Up:** Attempt to fold and store your deflated decorations. Spoiler alert: they'll never fold down to their original size. At best, you'll roll them into an oversized lump and hope they fit in the attic.

4. **Decide Their Fate:** Do you save them for next year or toss them out? After seeing Santa collapse in a heap of nylon, you might lean toward the latter.

Why It's Funny:

Watching your giant inflatable Santa shrink into a wrinkled, flat pile is both a sad and hilarious metaphor for the end of any party. It's the visual representation of post-holiday exhaustion—both for Santa and for you.

The Coconut Drink Dilemma

Overview:

Those cute coconut cups with the tiny umbrellas were a hit at your tropical Christmas party—until you woke up to realize you now have approximately 45 leftover coconut shells scattered around your house. Don't toss them just yet! We've got some ideas.

Ideas for Leftover Coconut Cups:

- **Mini Planters:** Drill a hole in the bottom and stick a succulent inside. Now, your Christmas coconuts live on as year-round decor!
- **Bird Feeders:** Hang them up in your backyard and watch the local wildlife embrace the tropics. Your house might become the number one vacation spot for neighborhood birds.
- **Pet Hats:** Feeling mischievous? Pop one of those coconut halves onto your pet's head and snap a photo. Instant internet fame guaranteed.

The Coconut Drink Dilemma

- **Random Storage:** Coconut shells are perfect for loose change, keys, or that candy cane you didn't finish. Functional *and* tropical!

Why It's Funny:

There's something inherently absurd about trying to figure out what to do with a bunch of leftover coconut cups, especially when your options range from bird feeders to pet accessories. It's all part of the post-party madness.

Dealing with the Leftover Decorations

Overview:

Those inflatable flamingos, pineapple string lights, and tiki masks were perfect for your tropical Christmas party. But now? They're just a reminder of the chaos that was. Time to decide what stays and what goes.

Disposal vs. Reuse:

- **Option 1: Store It:** Tell yourself you'll use it again next year. You probably won't, but pack it up anyway—you'll regret throwing it out when next Christmas rolls around.
- **Option 2: Re-Gift It:** Who wouldn't want an inflatable flamingo as a white elephant gift? The possibilities are endless for quirky re-gifting opportunities.
- **Option 3: Repurpose It:** Feeling crafty? Turn your flamingos into garden gnomes, your pineapple

Dealing with the Leftover Decorations

lights into permanent patio decor, and your tiki masks into "art."

Why It's Funny:

Convincing yourself you'll reuse your tropical Christmas decorations is the epitome of post-holiday denial. By this point, everything looks a little sad and out of place, but you just might hold onto it—because, you know, *next year*.

Cleaning up after your tropical Christmas bash may seem like a daunting task, but with a little humor (and possibly another piña colada), you can turn the chaos into comedy gold. From battling the endless sand invasion to bidding farewell to your deflated holiday crew, the key is to embrace the mess and laugh at the absurdity of it all. After all, the best memories often come from the most unexpected moments—especially the ones you have to clean up afterward!

Sand, Sunburn, and Santa's Hawaiian Shirt: You Survived the Madness!

Well, you made it. You survived. The inflatable Santa has been deflated (hopefully), the last of the piña coladas has been sipped, and you're probably still finding grains of sand in places sand *should never be*. But hey—what's a little chaos in the name of holiday fun, right?

If you followed even half of the advice in this book, congratulations—you've officially thrown a Christmas party like no other. Your guests are likely still recovering from the sight of reindeer in sunglasses and Mrs. Claus rocking a sunhat. And let's not forget the flamingo ornaments hanging where snowflakes once dangled. You turned Christmas on its head and brought the tropics into the heart of winter—and probably into every nook and cranny of your living room too.

But beyond the tipped palm trees, over-inflated Santas, and the lingering smell of pineapple, you did something incredible: you made people laugh. You created memories that will be retold every year, probably with the sentence, "Remember that time we went to a Christmas party, and Santa was wearing a Hawaiian shirt?" If that's not holiday magic, I don't know what is.

Sand, Sunburn, and Santa's Hawaiian Shirt: You Survived the Madness!

So, here we are at the end of this sun-soaked sleigh ride. The lights have dimmed, the tiki torches have gone out (hopefully not in flames), and the tropical tunes have faded into the background. But before you put this book away (and hopefully before you find one last bit of leftover coconut drink hiding in the fridge), take a moment to appreciate what you've done. You threw a party that defied the norm, broke tradition, and added a splash of sunshine to the holiday season.

Now, as you sit there in the aftermath—perhaps nursing a mild sunburn from your *indoor* luau—remember that Christmas, like life, is meant to be enjoyed. Whether it's with mistletoe and eggnog or flamingos and margaritas, the real magic is in the laughter, the shared chaos, and the unforgettable moments.

And who knows? Maybe you've just started a new tradition: Tropical Christmas 2.0, coming next year, bigger and better (and maybe with fewer inflatable reindeer casualties).

Until then, may your days be merry, your drinks be fruity, and your holiday spirit as bright as a flamingo covered in Christmas lights. Cheers to a tropical holiday like no other—and to all the wild, wonderful, and completely outrageous parties still to come.

Aloha, Merry Christmas, and see you next year! 🌴 🎅 🍹

From the Desk of Bree Winters: Surviving Christmas, One Piña Colada at a Time

Well, well, well. Look who made it to the *exclusive* behind-the-scenes chapter! Welcome to my desk, where the smell of sunscreen blends with cinnamon candles, and where Christmas playlists are played on steel drums (because why not?). If you're here, it means you've stuck with me through the palm tree tipping, inflatable reindeer disasters, and the great sand cleanup of 2023. First of all—congratulations. Second of all, what were you thinking?

I'm Bree Winters, your guide on this absurd, sun-drenched sleigh ride through a tropical Christmas wonderland. People often ask me, *"Bree, why tropical Christmas? What inspired you to throw palm trees into a holiday traditionally associated with snowmen and hot cocoa?"* And to that, I say: because chaos is fun, and Santa deserves a vacation, too.

Let me tell you a little secret about the making of this book: it was born from the rubble of my first-ever tropical-themed Christmas party, an event that still lives in infamy among my friends and family. Picture this: a flamingo tree topper that refused to stay upright, coconuts everywhere (seriously, *everywhere*), and

From the Desk of Bree Winters: Surviving Christmas, One Piña Colada ...

one unfortunate incident involving a tiki torch and someone's highly flammable sweater (no one was hurt, but my dignity took a hit).

As I watched my carefully planned tropical oasis devolve into a sea of inflatable Santas and spilled piña coladas, I had a moment of clarity: This is what Christmas should be—unpredictable, hilarious, and definitely *not* perfect. No one remembers the picture-perfect parties where everything goes according to plan. They remember the ones where Santa's flip-flop falls off, and the punch bowl somehow becomes a casualty of a rogue beach ball.

So, I decided to share that chaos with the world, and here we are.

This book is my love letter to the weird, wonderful moments that make the holidays unforgettable. It's not just a guide; it's an invitation to embrace the messiness, the mishaps, and the magic that happens when you mix mistletoe with margaritas. Sure, you'll probably end up with sand in your socks and a pineapple-scented house that won't quit, but isn't that what makes it all worth it?

I offer you this: permission to let go of the idea of a perfect Christmas. Instead, chase the version that's full of belly laughs, slightly questionable décor choices, and memories that make you smile long after the last ornament has been packed away.

So, if you're still considering whether or not to host a tropical Christmas next year, let me assure you: it will be messy, it will be loud, and it will probably go sideways at least once—but it will also be *epic*. And who knows? Maybe you'll start a new tradition, just like I did.

Now, if you'll excuse me, I've got an inflatable flamingo to deflate, a blender to clean, and—oh yes—a Christmas playlist featuring "Mele Kalikimaka" to put on repeat.

Merry Christmas, aloha, and may your holidays be as sunny, silly, and spectacular as you are.

From the Desk of Bree Winters: Surviving Christmas, One Piña Colada ...

With endless tropical cheer, **Bree Winters**
(*The self-appointed queen of Christmas chaos*)

40

www.ingramcontent.com/pod-product-compliance
Lightning Source LLC
LaVergne TN
LVHW050024080526
838202LV00069B/6906